THE Ultimate World Quiz

Written by Claire Llewellyn

Collins

Contents

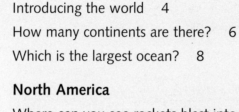

Africa

Asia

Oceania

Antarctica

Introducing the world

The world is a remarkable place. More than two-thirds of it is covered by oceans and seas. The rest of it is covered by dry land, with mountains, deserts, forests, plains and other fascinating features. People have added to the natural landscape, constructing towns and cities, monuments and other kinds of building.

This book is packed with facts about the world. Is the Sahara *really* the world's largest desert? Why is Antarctica colder than the Arctic? How did the Dead Sea get its name? Find the answers to these and other questions and become a walking encyclopedia of the four corners of the Earth.

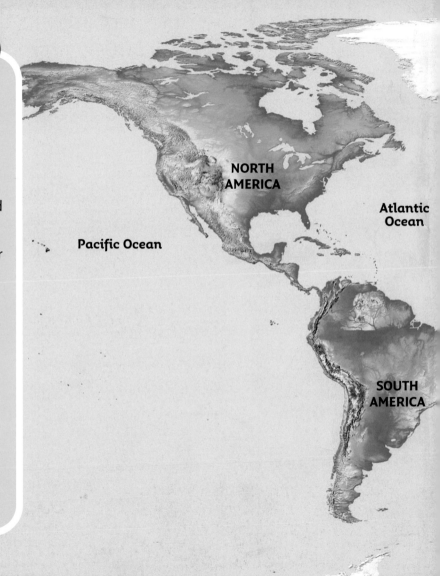

NORTH AMERICA

Atlantic Ocean

Pacific Ocean

SOUTH AMERICA

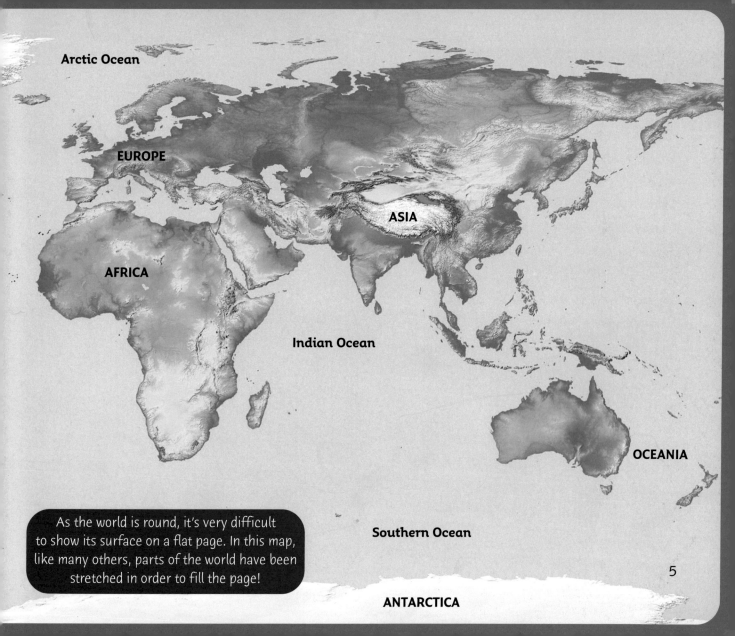

Arctic Ocean

EUROPE

ASIA

AFRICA

Indian Ocean

OCEANIA

As the world is round, it's very difficult
to show its surface on a flat page. In this map,
like many others, parts of the world have been
stretched in order to fill the page!

Southern Ocean

5

ANTARCTICA

How many continents are there?

Continents are massive pieces of land and there are *seven* of them altogether: North America, South America, Europe, Africa, Asia, Oceania and Antarctica. These continents didn't always look the way they do today. Scientists believe that about 250 million years ago all the continents were joined together in one huge piece of land. The scientists called the landmass Pangaea. Gradually Pangaea broke up to form different continents, which then slowly drifted apart. This is because they rest on the Earth's plates – huge pieces of our planet's crust – which float on hot, **molten** rock deep inside the Earth.

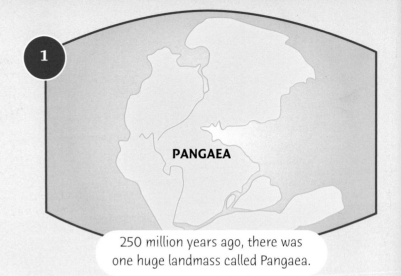

1

PANGAEA

250 million years ago, there was one huge landmass called Pangaea.

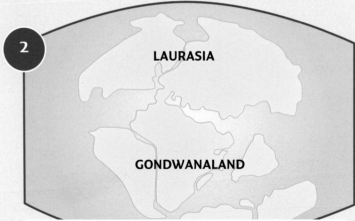

2

LAURASIA

GONDWANALAND

About 180 million years ago, Pangaea began to break up. First, there were two great landmasses - Laurasia in the north, and Gondwanaland in the south. These then split to form two further landmasses - Laurentia and Eurasia.

3

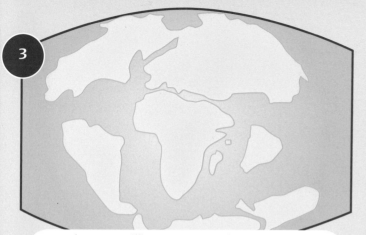

About 65 million years ago, the continents broke into smaller pieces and moved further apart.

4

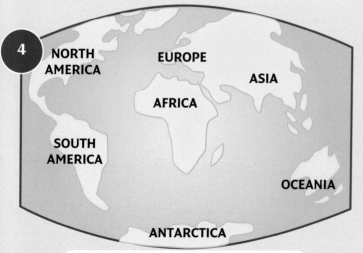

NORTH AMERICA
EUROPE
ASIA
AFRICA
SOUTH AMERICA
OCEANIA
ANTARCTICA

Today, the continents look like this.

This table shows the continents in order of size.

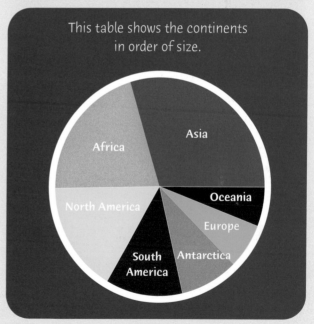

Asia
Africa
Oceania
North America
Europe
South America
Antarctica

Which is the largest ocean?

There are five oceans in the world – the Pacific, the Atlantic, the Indian, the Southern and the Arctic. Of these, the *Pacific* is by far the largest – bigger than the other four put together. The Pacific covers over one-third of the Earth's surface, stretching from the shores of Asia and Australia to the Americas and Antarctica. It contains more than half of all the world's liquid water.

Pacific Ocean

The blue planet: this picture of the Earth, taken from space, shows the vastness of the Pacific Ocean.

At the bottom of the Pacific lies the ocean floor. Far from being flat and boring, it's made up of rolling plains, high mountains and deep valleys.

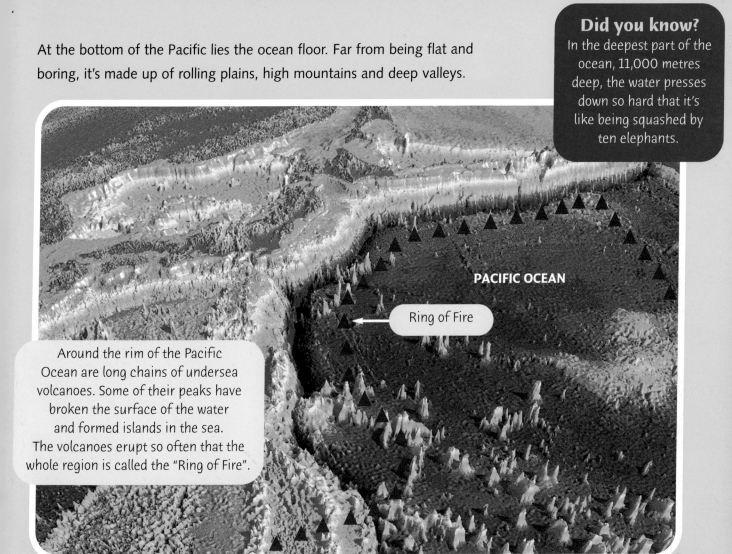

PACIFIC OCEAN

Ring of Fire

Around the rim of the Pacific Ocean are long chains of undersea volcanoes. Some of their peaks have broken the surface of the water and formed islands in the sea. The volcanoes erupt so often that the whole region is called the "Ring of Fire".

9

North America

Where can you see rockets blast into space?

On the coast of Florida, in southeast USA, there is a **headland** called *Cape Canaveral* that sticks out into the sea. It's home to the John F Kennedy Space Centre, the famous space launch site of NASA (the National Aeronautics and Space Administration). It's from here that space shuttles, rockets, satellites and **probes** are launched into outer space. The Centre has seen many famous missions, such as the Apollo 11 Moon launch, in 1969, carrying Neil Armstrong, the first man to walk on the Moon.

USA

Cape Canaveral •

10

11

Did you know?
Part of the Space Centre site is a wildlife refuge, and alligators often sun themselves on the runway at Cape Canaveral. Staff have to check for stray alligators before a space shuttle comes in to land.

Which is the largest gorge in the world?

A gorge is a deep, narrow valley that has been cut by a river and the largest one lies in northern Arizona in the USA. It's called the *Grand Canyon* and measures 446 kilometres long, up to 18 kilometres wide and 1.8 kilometres deep. This huge gorge was slow in the making; it has been carved out by the Colorado River during the last ten million years.

USA

• Grand Canyon

Did you know?
Over four million people visit the Grand Canyon each year. They fly along it in a helicopter, float down the river on a raft or explore it on foot or on the back of a mule.

The walls of the Grand Canyon are made of rock. The oldest rock layers at the bottom of the gorge are nearly two billion years old. The youngest layers at the top are "only" 200 million years old. The rocks contain ancient fossils, the remains of plants and animals that once lived on the Earth. The oldest rock contains fossils of some of the first plants ever to live in the sea while the younger rock contains fossils of early animals, including fish, insects and reptiles.

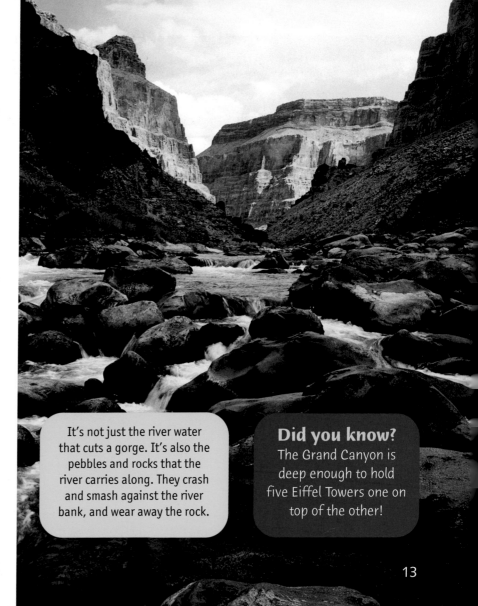

It's not just the river water that cuts a gorge. It's also the pebbles and rocks that the river carries along. They crash and smash against the river bank, and wear away the rock.

Did you know?
The Grand Canyon is deep enough to hold five Eiffel Towers one on top of the other!

Which are the longest mountains in the world?

Many people think that the world's longest mountains are the Andes in South America. Well, they're wrong! There's a much longer mountain chain that stretches a distance of about 16,000 kilometres – almost from the North Pole to the South Pole. This chain of mountains lies hidden on the sea bed under the Atlantic Ocean and it's known as the *mid-Atlantic ridge*.

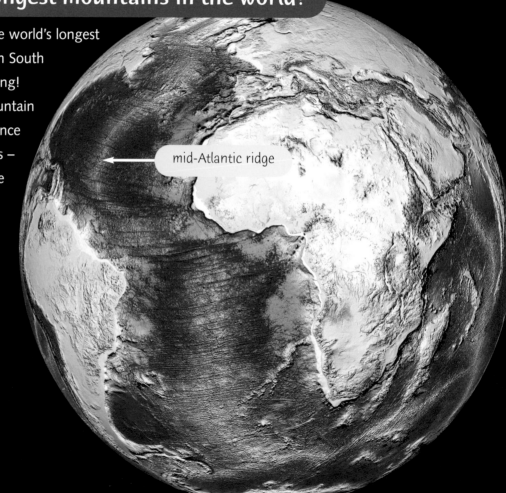

mid-Atlantic ridge

A ridge is a mountain chain that forms where two of the Earth's plates meet. Sometimes the plates move apart, and when they do, molten rock known as lava forces its way up and into the sea. The lava cools as it meets the cold water, and soon sets into solid rock on the ocean floor. As more and more lava erupts and hardens, a chain of underwater mountains is built along the edges of the plates. Iceland was formed in this way. It's one of the few places where the mid-Atlantic ridge can be seen above the sea.

The Andes mountains are the longest mountain chain on land. They stretch 7,200 kilometres from the tropical north of South America to its icy tip in the south. Hidden in the Andes are ancient cities, such as Machu Picchu, which was built by a people called the Incas 500 years ago.

Did you know?
In 1963 molten rock welled up from the mid-Atlantic ridge and formed the tiny island of Surtsey, off Iceland's southern coast. Iceland was formed in the same way about 20 million years ago.

15

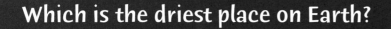

Which is the driest place on Earth?

The *Atacama desert*, along the coast of northern Chile, is the driest place on the Earth. In some parts rain has never been recorded, while in others it hasn't rained for decades or centuries. Few things can live in this hostile place; you won't see a blade of grass or a lizard or a gnat.

Did you know?
Arica, a town in the Atacama desert, gets just 0.76 millimetres of rain per year. At that rate it would take a century to fill a small coffee cup.

16

The desert is roughly the size of Switzerland. Its harsh landscape is made of hardened lava flows, sun-baked rock, sand and piles of salt, which form strange, statue-like shapes. The landscape resembles the surface of the Moon, so when scientists were developing a lunar rover – a vehicle for astronauts to use on the Moon – they decided to test it here!

Some of the world's oldest **mummies** have been found in the Atacama desert. They have been perfectly preserved by the dry desert air. People have lived in this part of Chile for over 4,000 years.

Which is the biggest rainforest?

The *Amazon rainforest* in South America is the biggest tropical forest in the world. Its vast **canopy** stretches across the top of the continent, from the Andes mountains in the west to the Atlantic Ocean in the east. The rainforest grows in the basin of the Amazon River. This river is over 6,500 kilometres long, and carries one-fifth of the world's fresh water.

Amazon rainforest

SOUTH AMERICA

Did you know?
In some places and in different seasons, the Amazon River floods its banks. The forest is "drowned" in up to 20 metres of water, allowing fish, crocodiles and anaconda snakes to swim among the trees.

18

The rainforest is home to more than one million plant and animal **species**. Many rainforest plants provide us with food – Brazil nuts, avocados and ginger, for example. The forest also provides rubber and wood, and medicines that fight disease.

Plants take in carbon dioxide from the air. They use the gas inside their leaves to make food that helps them grow. During this process, the leaves give out oxygen – the gas we breathe in and need to survive. The Amazon rainforest produces about 20% of the Earth's oxygen.

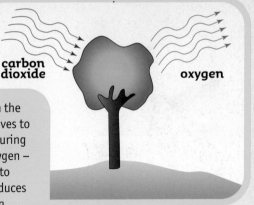

carbon dioxide

oxygen

19

Europe

Where is the land of the Midnight Sun?

Lapland

EUROPE

The *far north of Scandinavia*, a region called Lapland, is known as the land of the Midnight Sun. This is because, in midsummer, the sun hardly dips below the **horizon**, and the sky stays light all through the night – excellent for all-night sledging. Unfortunately, in winter, the opposite is true. From mid-November to mid-January, the sun doesn't rise above the horizon and the days are dark and gloomy. Children walk, or ski, to school by the light of the moon and stars.

This region lies deep inside the Arctic Circle. It's home to the Sami, the native people who have lived there for centuries. In the past, they lived by hunting and fishing and following herds of wild reindeer, which provided them with meat, milk and skins. Today, there are about 85,000 Sami and, although most of them now have more ordinary jobs, some of them still raise reindeer, which are domesticated rather than wild.

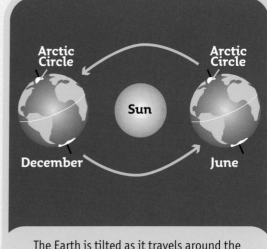

The Earth is tilted as it travels around the Sun. In June, the Arctic Circle leans towards the Sun and the days are long and light. In December, the Arctic Circle leans away from the Sun and the days are short and dark.

Which countries are joined under the sea?

The *United Kingdom (UK) and France* are only 34 kilometres apart. For centuries, the two countries were divided by the English Channel, and the only way to cross was by boat or plane. Now they are linked by a rail tunnel that runs deep under the sea.

UK

English — Channel

FRANCE

The huge engineering project began in 1987. Three tunnels were dug – one for trains to France, one for trains to the UK, and a third "service" tunnel to provide access to the other two. All the tunnels were dug through the sea bed, a chalky rock that formed in the distant past when dinosaurs were still alive.

The Channel Tunnel opened in May 1994. Trains travel through it every day, transporting people, cars and coaches to the other side. The trains travel at up to 160 kilometres per hour and the journey time through the tunnel is about 35 minutes.

The Channel tunnels were cut with tunnel boring machines (TBMs). The cutting face of a TBM contains 100 revolving blades and 200 sharp biting teeth, which cut through the ground at an average rate of 1.6 kilometres per hour. The tunnel was bored under the sea bed up to a depth of 75 metres below the channel floor.

In which city are the streets filled with water?

The Italian city of *Venice* is unique. It's built on over 100 tiny islands which lie inside a lagoon, a sheltered area of sea water almost cut off from the open sea. In-between the islands are canals, and it's these that form the city's "streets". To get from one part of Venice to another, you either go on foot – using the hundreds of bridges that crisscross the canals – or go by boat.

Venice•

Italy

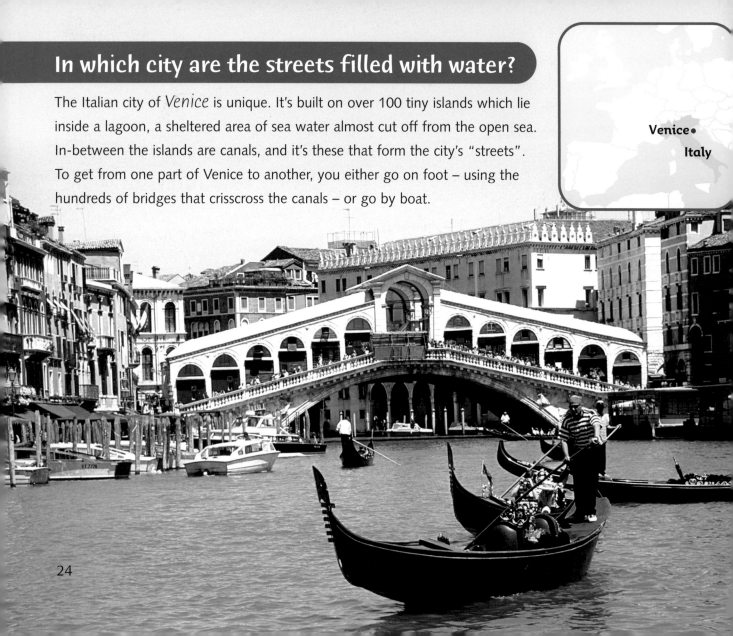

About 500 years ago, Venice was a wealthy and powerful trading city and many fine squares and churches were built. The richest merchants lived in palaces along the busy canals. Visitors and goods arrived by gondolas, the traditional, flat-bottomed boats that are still used in Venice today.

Did you know?
Venice is famous for its annual carnival. The Venetians wear elaborate costumes and face masks.

The sea level is slowly rising because of climate change. As a result, parts of Venice can be flooded during winter and **Venetians** have to walk on platforms above the water-logged streets.

Africa

Where can you see Africa's spectacular herds?

The *Serengeti plains* in northwest Tanzania are a huge area of tropical grassland, roughly the size of Wales. The rolling **plains** are home to herds of animals, including wildebeest, elephants, zebras and gazelles, which feed on the grasses and thorny shrubs and trees.

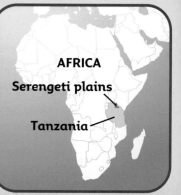

AFRICA
Serengeti plains

Tanzania

26

The Serengeti lies close to the equator. This area has a tropical climate with two main seasons – rainy and dry. In the rainy season, the animals graze widely over the plains. In the dry season, they form large herds made up of hundreds of thousands of animals. The herds **migrate** huge distances, searching for fresh grass and drinking water. The animals are themselves a source of food for lions, leopards, cheetahs, hyenas and other hungry **predators**.

Did you know?
The Serengeti is home to a tribe called the Masai. They herd cattle, goats and sheep and collect plants from the wild.

The animals that graze on the Serengeti drop colossal amounts of dung. It's tidied away by dung beetles, which roll it into their underground nests and feed it to their young.

Which is the world's longest river?

The *River Nile* is the longest river in the world. It begins at Lake Victoria in Uganda and flows 6,695 kilometres to the Mediterranean Sea. In Egypt, at the end of its journey, the river flows so slowly that the fine mud it is carrying sinks to the river bed. Over millions of years, the mud has piled up to form fertile land in the mouth of the river. This is called a delta.

The world's longest rivers
1: Nile, Africa, 6,695 kilometres
2: Amazon, South America, 6,516 kilometres
3: Yangtze, Asia, 6,380 kilometres

The ancient Egyptians began farming here about 8,000 years ago. The harvests were so abundant that the country grew rich, and built a great civilisation. The Egyptian rulers, the pharaohs, built stone temples and tombs, which have survived until the present day. Egyptians still farm the Nile delta. It's a lush, green landscape that's very different from the rest of Egypt's **arid** land.

Did you know?
River deltas got their name because most of them are triangular in shape, and look like "delta", the fourth letter of the Greek alphabet.

Boats called feluccas have sailed on the Nile for thousands of years. Feluccas have one broad, triangular sail.

29

Where is the biggest building made of mud?

In *Djenné* (pronounced jay-NAY), a small city in Mali, West Africa, there is a huge mosque built of sun-dried mud. Known as the Great Mosque, it's the biggest mud-built structure in the world. Building with mud may sound primitive but Mali masons are well trained and produce beautiful constructions. Besides, it makes good sense to build with local, natural materials.

Mali

• Djenné

AFRICA

There has been a mosque in Djenné for hundreds of years, for the town was an important trading centre and a place of Islamic pilgrimage and learning. The Great Mosque, completed in 1907, was constructed on a raised platform, which protects the building from the annual flooding of the nearby river. The high walls, built of mud bricks called adobe, need to be 60 centimetres thick to carry the weight of the building. They insulate the prayer halls from the heat of the day and the bitter cold of night.

Did you know?
On top of each of the Mosque's three towers is a spire capped with an ostrich egg. The eggs are a symbol of fertility and purity.

Rain can easily damage mud buildings. To avoid this, gutter pipes have been added all around the Mosque. They allow rain to run off the roof without pouring down the walls and washing them away.

Every year, during a springtime festival, the Great Mosque is re-plastered and restored. Local townspeople swarm to the Mosque, supplying the masons with buckets of water and soft, sticky mud. The masons balance on palm wood beams, which were added to the walls during construction to help prevent the mud from cracking.

Asia

Which is the world's deepest lake?

Lake Baikal lies in central Russia just north of the border with Mongolia. It measures 636 kilometres long, up to 80 kilometres wide, and over 1,600 metres deep – deep enough to swallow Ben Nevis, the highest mountain in the British Isles. This makes it the world's deepest lake. It also contains more water than any other lake in the world.

Russia   Lake Baikal

ASIA

Did you know?
Scientists have calculated that it would take all the world's rivers a whole year to fill Lake Baikal.

Lake Baikal is a crescent-shaped lake, surrounded by mountains and forests. The Russians call it "the blue eye of Siberia", the region in which it is found.

The local people, the Tartars, named the huge body of water "Bai-Ku", which means "rich lake". It's a good name for these pure waters, which scientists have called one of the biological wonders of the world. This is because they are home to about 1,800 different animal species, many of which, including a freshwater seal, are found nowhere else in the world. The abundant lake provides food for people. In winter, when the surface freezes over, the locals cut holes in the ice so they can continue to fish in the water below.

Winters in Siberia are bitterly cold.
From January to May, Lake Baikal freezes over.
The surface ice is 120 centimetres thick –
thick enough to drive across in a loaded truck.

33

Where is the longest wall in the world?

Can you imagine a wall so long that it would stretch from London in the UK to Chicago in the USA? Well, the *Great Wall of China* is just such a wall. It stretches about 6,400 kilometres through the mountains and deserts of northern China. It's the longest wall in the world.

Great Wall of China

China

ASIA

Did you know?
It's often said that the Great Wall of China can be seen from the Moon. This is untrue, although the Wall can be seen by satellites far above the Earth.

The enormous structure was built by slaves. Work on it began over 2,200 years ago by order of the first Chinese emperor, Shi Huangdi. He hoped that the Wall would keep out invaders who threatened China from the north. Later emperors continued the work on the Wall. In truth, it's not one single wall, but a number of different walls joined together. Along its length are 25,000 square watchtowers. These were manned by Chinese guards, who watched the desolate hills for signs of danger. Signals were sent to warn of an attack – either by smoke, during the day, or by fire, at night.

The Great Wall of China is made of two vertical walls sandwiched together with soil and rubble. The top is about four metres wide and was paved with stone slabs. This created a useful roadway to move troops, or soldiers on horseback, from one place to another.

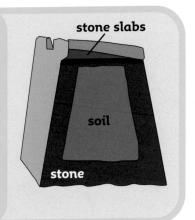

stone slabs

soil

stone

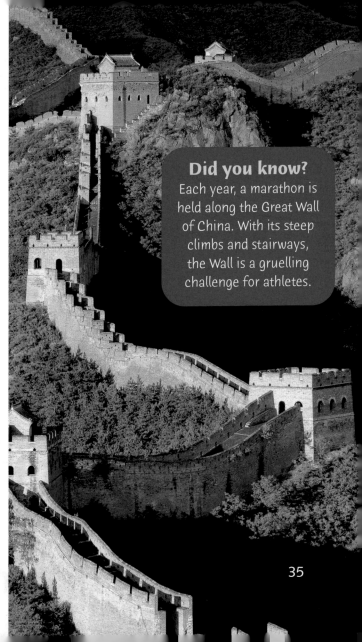

Did you know?
Each year, a marathon is held along the Great Wall of China. With its steep climbs and stairways, the Wall is a gruelling challenge for athletes.

In which sea is it almost impossible to sink?

The *Dead Sea*, which is actually a lake, lies between Israel and Jordan in the Middle East. The water in the lake is very salty, much saltier than the sea. The high salt content makes the water very dense so that swimming in it is a strange sensation: it's almost impossible to sink!

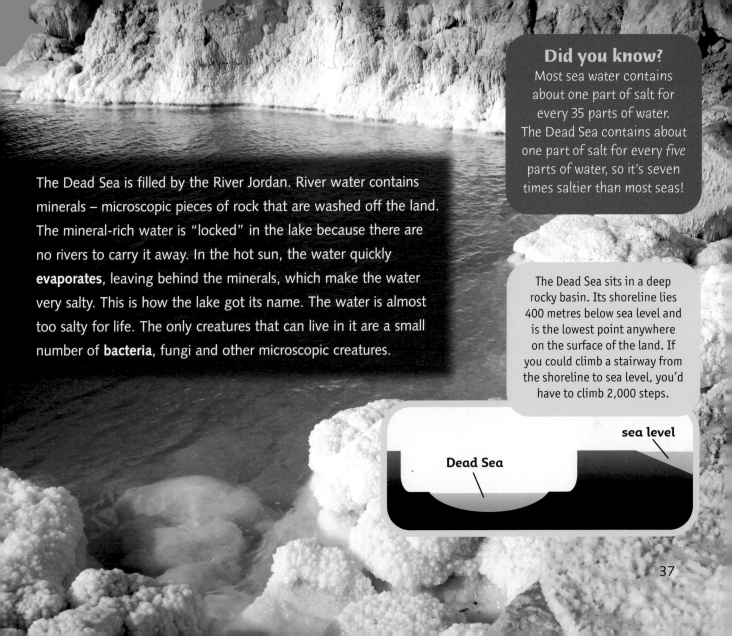

Most sea water contains about one part of salt for every 35 parts of water. The Dead Sea contains about one part of salt for every *five* parts of water, so it's seven times saltier than most seas!

The Dead Sea is filled by the River Jordan. River water contains minerals – microscopic pieces of rock that are washed off the land. The mineral-rich water is "locked" in the lake because there are no rivers to carry it away. In the hot sun, the water quickly **evaporates**, leaving behind the minerals, which make the water very salty. This is how the lake got its name. The water is almost too salty for life. The only creatures that can live in it are a small number of **bacteria**, fungi and other microscopic creatures.

The Dead Sea sits in a deep rocky basin. Its shoreline lies 400 metres below sea level and is the lowest point anywhere on the surface of the land. If you could climb a stairway from the shoreline to sea level, you'd have to climb 2,000 steps.

sea level

Dead Sea

Which is the world's highest mountain?

Everyone thinks that Mount Everest is the world's highest mountain, but there's another one that's even higher! It's a volcano called *Mauna Kea*, which forms part of the island of Hawaii about 3,900 kilometres off the southwest coast of the USA. Mauna Kea sits on the sea bed deep under the Pacific Ocean. From there, it rises 10,205 metres, about 1,300 metres higher than Mount Everest. Its top breaks the surface of the water, forming an island whose snow-capped summit is 4,205 metres above sea level.

Pacific Ocean

USA

Hawaii
• **Mauna Kea**

Did you know?
Mauna Kea's most recent eruption was about 4,500 years ago.

The atmosphere above the summit is dry, clear, free from clouds and a long way from any kind of light pollution. This makes it the perfect place for the world's largest observatory. At night astronomers work the telescopes, peering through the dark, crystal-clear skies to observe the stars, planets and galaxies of outer space.

Did you know?
Thirteen telescopes have been built on the top of Mauna Kea. They belong to 11 different countries, whose astronomers work and study there.

The highest mountain in each continent (on land):

Oceania:
Mauna Kea
10,205 metres total
4,205 metres
above sea level

Asia:
Mt Everest
8,848 metres

South America:
Aconcagua
6,959 metres

North America:
Mt McKinley
6,194 metres

Africa:
Mt Kilimanjaro
5,895 metres

Europe:
Mt Elbrus
5,633 metres

Antarctica:
Vinson Massif
5,139 metres

Oceania:
Mt Kosciusko
2,230 metres

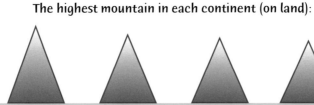

Which is the largest rock in the world?

In the middle of the Australian outback stands a massive sandstone rock. It rises 348 metres above the sandy plain, and is more than nine kilometres around. It is called *Uluru*, an Aboriginal name meaning "Great Pebble". Formed 500 million years ago, Uluru is the world's largest single rock. It's even larger than it appears for, like an iceberg, only its tip can be seen – a further six kilometres of the rock extends below the ground.

AUSTRALIA
• **Uluru**

Running water has worn away Uluru's surface, cutting ridges and furrows, hollows and caves. The local Aboriginals used the caves as shelters for many thousands of years, and their ancient paintings can be seen on the walls. Uluru is sacred to the Aboriginals. For this reason, climbing the rock is discouraged and, anyway, it's gruelling in summer when the average temperature is 38° centigrade.

Uluru is made of different minerals. These change colour as the light strikes the rock at different times of the day and the year. It can appear blue or violet, while at sunrise or sunset it's a glowing red.

41

Where do jets of boiling water shoot out of the ground?

Near *Rotorua*, a town on New Zealand's North Island, spectacular jets of steaming water erupt out of the ground. The jets, known as geysers, shoot up to a height of 30 metres up to 20 times a day. Each eruption lasts a few minutes before the water sinks back down into a hole in the ground.

How are the geysers made? Rotorua lies in an area of volcanic activity, and the rocks close to the Earth's surface are very, very hot. As rainwater trickles down and collects between the rocks, it's heated like water in a kettle. Soon, it boils and is forced upwards through cracks in the ground.

North Island

NEW ZEALAND

• Rotorua

South Island

In some places, the water flows out gently as hot springs. In others, it bubbles through a layer of clay, making boiling mud pools. Many of the visitors to Rotorua believe that minerals in the water give it miraculous healing properties. They like to soak in the hot springs and cover their face and body with the "precious" mud.

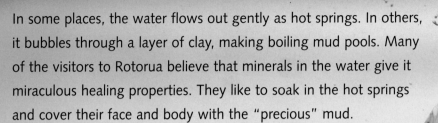

Did you know?
In volcanic areas, strong-smelling gases leak out of the ground. The air in places like Rotorua stinks of rotten eggs!

The boiling hot water under the ground dissolves the rock around it. Because of this, geyser water contains tiny pieces of rock called minerals. When the geyser shoots out and the water cools down, these minerals pile up on the ground and make unusual rock formations.

43

Antarctica

Which is the world's largest desert?

ANTARCTICA

Many people think that the Sahara Desert is the largest desert in the world. However, *Antarctica* is one-and-a-half times bigger than the Sahara, and much of it is also a desert. Deserts are not always hot. For example, the Gobi Desert in northern Asia has winters that are icy cold. Deserts are places where the total rainfall (including snow, sleet or hail) is less than 25 centimetres a year. Antarctica is so cold that, in many parts of the continent, it's just too cold to snow. This makes it a vast frozen desert.

44

45

Most of the land in Antarctica is covered with ice up to five kilometres thick. However, in one area, known as the Dry Valleys, the land is bare rock. No snow has covered it for millions of years. Any flakes are blasted by dry winds that suck the moisture away, making these valleys one of the driest places on Earth.

The Dry Valleys were discovered by the British explorer, Captain Robert Scott, in 1903. The ice-free surface was a nasty surprise for him and his men. They were pulling sledges, loaded with equipment, that would not slide over the bare rock. Eventually the expedition was forced to turn around.

Which is the coldest place in the world?

Vostok Station is a Russian scientific research station that lies in east Antarctica nearly 3,500 metres above sea level. In summer, the average temperature is -30° centigrade, while in winter it is usually around -65° centigrade. One winter night, the thermometer sank to -89.6° centigrade, the lowest temperature ever recorded on the Earth!

AFRICA

SOUTH AMERICA

ANTARCTICA

•Vostok

AUSTRALIA

Compare the temperature at Vostok Station with other places on the Earth

| Lowest on Earth: Vostok Station east Antarctica -89.6 centigrade (on 21/7/1983) | Lowest in UK: Altnaharra, Scottish Highlands – -27.2° centigrade (on 30/12/1995) | Highest in UK: Faversham, Kent – 38.5° centigrade (on 10/8/2003) | Highest on Earth: Al' Azizyah, Libya – 57.8° centigrade (on 13/9/1922) |

Scientists at Vostok and other research stations drill holes into the thick ice sheet and bring out samples called ice cores. The ice, from a depth of over four kilometres, contains bubbles of air which carry clues about the Earth's climate in the past. They show changes in the temperature, changes in the air, and even contain dust from volcanic eruptions. This helps scientists to understand about the way the Earth's climate has changed over the past 400,000 years. It may also help them to understand how the climate may change in the future.

In 1996 scientists at Vostok discovered a vast lake of fresh, liquid water deep under the Antarctic ice. The water has been sealed from the rest of the planet for at least 15 million years. It may be home to forms of life found nowhere else on the Earth. The scientists are trying to find a way to enter the lake without polluting the water.

ice

Lake Vostok   rock

Well done! You've finished this book and reached the end of the ultimate world quiz. You've scaled mountains, explored forests and dived under the sea. You've visited Antarctica, sailed along the Nile and climbed the Great Wall of China.

But why stop here? Finding out about the world is a lifelong adventure, so keep on exploring the Earth – not only on buses, boats and trains but also in books, maps, on the Internet and in travel programmes on TV. And when you meet people who have visited or lived in other parts of the world, ask them questions about these places and all the things they've seen. Knowledge about the world is a great adventure and there is much, much more to learn.

Good luck!

The world in numbers

Estimated age:	4.6 billion years
World population:	About 6.4 billion people

Surface area:	510 million sq km
Land area:	149 million sq km
Total water area:	361 million sq km (97% salt water; 3% fresh water)

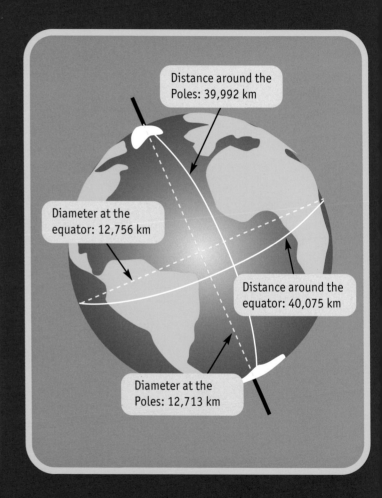

Distance around the Poles: 39,992 km

Diameter at the equator: 12,756 km

Distance around the equator: 40,075 km

Diameter at the Poles: 12,713 km

Largest countries by area:		
1	Russian Federation	17,075,400 sq km
2	Canada	9,984,670 sq km
3	USA	9,826,635 sq km
4	China	9,584,492 sq km

Countries with largest population:		
1	China	1,323 million
2	India	1,103 million
3	USA	298 million
4	Indonesia	245 million

Glossary

arid	very dry and with few signs of life
bacteria	microscopic living things
canopy	the top layer of a forest, made up of the branches and leaves of the trees
evaporates	changes from a liquid into a gas, such as when water dries up and seems to disappear
headland	a piece of land that sticks out into the sea
horizon	the line where the earth and the sky seem to meet
migrate	to travel from one place to another at certain times of the year
molten	melted
mummies	dead human or animal bodies that have been preserved
plains	large areas of fairly flat land
predators	animals that kill other animals for food
probes	unmanned spacecrafts that travel through space and send back information to Earth
species	kinds of animals or plants
Venetians	the natives of Venice

Index

Review

This world map is marked with the places featured in the book.

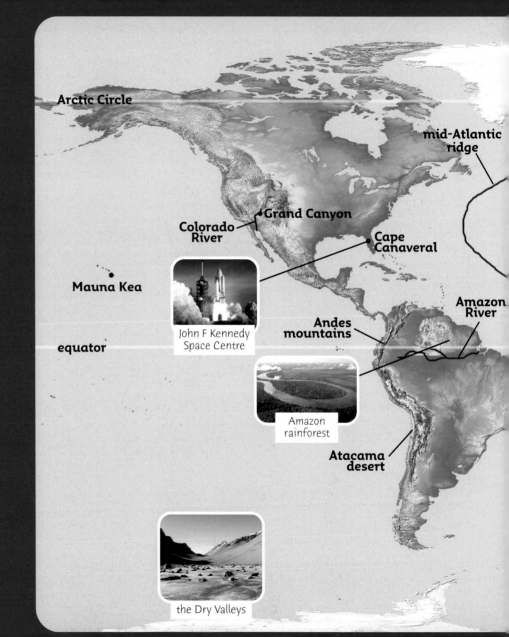

Arctic Circle

mid-Atlantic ridge

Grand Canyon

Colorado River

Cape Canaveral

Mauna Kea

Amazon River

Andes mountains

John F Kennedy Space Centre

equator

Amazon rainforest

Atacama desert

the Dry Valleys

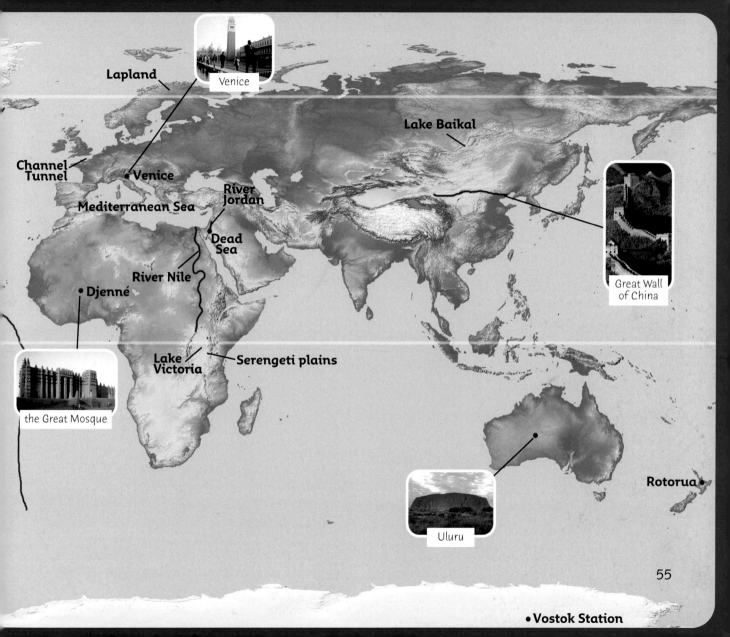

Lapland

Venice

Lake Baikal

Channel
Tunnel

•Venice

River
Jordan

Mediterranean Sea

Dead
Sea

Great Wall
of China

River Nile

•Djenné

Lake
Victoria

Serengeti plains

the Great Mosque

Uluru

Rotorua•

55

•Vostok Station

✿ Ideas for guided reading ✿

Learning objectives: make notes on a text to explain ideas; compare different types of information text and identify how they are structured; use and explore different question types

Curriculum links: Geography: Passport to the world

Interest words: arid, canopy, headland, migrate, molten, plains, probes

Resources: globe, notebooks

Getting started

This book can be read over two or more guided reading sessions.

- Read the front cover and the blurb together and try to answer the three questions.

- Ask children to predict what this book is about and what it might be used for.

- Read the contents together. Help children decode tricky new words (e.g. Oceania) and remind them about strategies for tackling new and tricky words (e.g. phonics, looking for words within the word, using context, using grammar cues).

- In pairs, raise and record two more questions about the world.

Reading and responding

- Read pp4–5 together. Ask children to recount a fact that they have read.

- Look at the world map and try to identify some known places. Discuss what is known about these places (e.g. climate, industry, physical features).

- Read pp6–9. Model how to note three interesting facts in a practical way.

- Explain that the book is organised by continent. Ask children to choose a continent, read about it and make brief notes to help them recall key facts to share with the group.